SOUTH

Images of America
. . .by the world's greatest photographers.

The "Olde Pink House" tavern and restaurant. Savannah, Georgia.

A yellow Corvette blends with the bright sun and frolic of Florida's Ft. Lauderdale Beach.

The booming city of Birmingham, Alabama, glows on a clear summer's night.

"Capt. Sam" Stevens of Savannah, Georgia.

SOUTH

Images of America

. . . by the world's greatest photographers.

GALLERY BOOKS

An Imprint of W. H. Smith Publishers Inc.
112 Madison Avenue
New York City 10016

THE IMAGE BANK®

111 Fifth Avenue
New York, N.Y. 10003

First published 1986 in New York by Gallery
Books, an imprint of W.H. Smith Publishers Inc.,
112 Madison Avenue, New York, N.Y. 10016

ISBN 0-8317-7927-6

For rights information about the photographs in
this book please contact:

The Image Bank
111 Fifth Avenue, New York, N.Y. 10003

Manufactured in Singapore

Produced by Robert M. Tod
Art Directed/Designed by Michael T. Connelly
Written/Edited by Michael O'Connor
Photo Research: Amy Jaffe, Kim Lee Kahn

"Poets have done better in expressing the oneness
of the South than historians have done in explaining it."

— James G. Randall

The "South" is defined by <u>Webster's New World Dictionary of the American Language</u> as "that part of the United States which is bordered on the north by the southern border of Penn., the Ohio river, the eastern and northern borders of Missouri; specific in the Civil War, the Confederacy."

But, as the historian Francis Butler Simkin so beautifully stated, "the South is an attitude of mind and a way of behavior just as much as it is a territory."

The American South is much more than a geographical region of the United States. It is a way of life. It is an outlook and approach, a rich and varied culture, a long and proud history — more than it is a specific group of States.

The South is a crucial component of America's culture. One of the things which makes America unique — a region and a way of life which is entirely American. The South's long history, its present pockets of prosperity and its present pockets of poverty, its potential for the future — all intertwine with, and influence, the rest of the country and the continent. The South is a component of America's heritage, and an important part of America's future.

In many ways the South is an extensive universe — without tight and definite boundaries. While some people speak of the South as the specific states which formed the Confederacy and fought against the North in the Civil War, others define the South by geographic boundaries such as rivers and mountain chains, or by climatic conditions. Neither group is really right, for the South blends, combines, and merges into other regions of America in an almost seamless pattern.

The influence of the South, and the Southern way of thinking or acting, subtly extends well beyond specific geographic borders and into every corner of the continent of North America. The South can be found in New York and Seattle, as well as in Mobile, Alabama.

The South is not a homogeneous subject which can easily be categorized. Rather, it is a crazy-quilt patchwork — a kaleidoscope of contrasts and combinations. A gigantic jigsaw puzzle with an almost endless number of pieces, each cut in a different but detailed pattern, and each matching with all the others in infinite ways.

No single book — indeed, no extensive encyclopedia of multiple volumes — can do justice to the universe of the South. It cannot cover all the subjects, discuss all the influences, even offer a good overall outline. All a single book can do is come in tight on one small aspect — or offer brief glimpses into parts of the larger picture of the South.

What this book attempts to do is offer a selection of striking images of today's South — a glimpse at a few factors, a few feelings out of the scope of sensations. We can only flash a few faces out of millions. We can only sketch out the briefest skeleton. We can only impart but a few facts. We can only begin to touch upon but fraction of the highlights.

But, that is fitting — for the South is the land of subjective sensations, of feelings and faces, of fragrances and emotions. It is the land of images and glimpses, of photographs, and slices of a gigantic picture.

The land of cotton. The land of tobacco, horses, peanuts, and Cajun blackened redfish. The land of vulcan factories firing steel through the night, and the land of textile mills clothing America. The home of Thomas Jefferson, Robert E. Lee, and the Reverend Martin Luther King. The land of historic houses, revered battlefields, and man's quest to conquer the challenge of space. The home of socially conscious "belles," and striving upwardly mobile yuppies.

The South is the home of Elvis Presley, Dixieland Jazz, negro spirituals, and New Orleans boogie-woogie. The land of guitar strumin' and banjo pickin' country boys. The birthplace of rock and roll. The heart of country music. The Grand Ole Opry, Graceland, Bourbon Street, and the Latin pulse of Miami.

The key to today's South may be found in the corridors of history. Perhaps the possibilities of the future lie there as well. The vitality and warmth may be found from the banks of the Potomac to the shores of the Gulf of Mexico.

Some say the South begins with Virginia — the land of Robert E. Lee, Thomas Jefferson, and the world's finest tobacco. Virginia, the state of George Washington and his beloved home Mt. Vernon.

Nestled on the Potomac river just across from the nation's capital, Washington, D.C., is the atmospheric and historic town of Alexandria. Once an important port, and now largely a "bedroom" community for the city of Washington and surrounding areas, Alexandria contains numerous beautifully and authentically maintained old private houses. A number of downtown streets are still paved with the original cobble stones. Downtown Alexandria contains the torpedo factory — once center of the U.S. Navy's early development and manufacturing of torpedoes. Today, the facility is a thriving art center filled with craftsmen's studios, galleries, and stores — the centerpiece of a revitalized and vibrant waterfront. It is somehow fitting that a building once devoted to the destruction of other men is now a tribute to aesthetic endeavor and the humanistic importance of art and craftsmanship.

Richmond, some 100 miles south of Alexandria, is the state capital of Virginia. Here, in historic St. John's Church, Patrick Henry spoke the famous words "give me liberty or give me death." Here, he declared the motto and the credo of the new nation, The United States of America.

Further south, and to the east, are the seacoast towns of Newport News and Norfolk, location of one of the United States most important naval bases — the world's largest naval base. Battleships, aircraft carriers, cruisers, and tenders — all painted the same grey, all self contained cities at sea.

Inland, almost smack in the middle of Virginia is the town of Appomattox — site of the famous battle which finally ended the tragic Civil War. It was on the fields near Appomattox that General Robert E. Lee surrendered to General Ulysses S. Grant of the Union army. Lee, one of the most important sons of Virginia, is fittingly buried on the campus of Washington and Lee University — an institution of higher learning dedicated to the future of America, and also to the heritage of our past.

The state of North Carolina butts up against Virginia's southeastern border. On the coast, North Carolina's long seashore curves down and out like the breast of a proud beast. Here, on the beaches outside a town with the forbidding name of Kill Devil Hills, Orville and Wilber Wright gambled on their rickety contraption — and conquered man's age-old quest for flight. Below Kill

Devil, Cape Hatteras and Cape Lookout National Seashores stretch like a long and fragile ribbon arching along the coast. Each year they offer enjoyment to millions of fishermen, tourists, and beach lovers.

In Asheville, North Carolina, you can visit Thomas Wolfe's boyhood home, and experience the city immortalized in his famous novel "Look Homeward Angel." North Carolina's literary heritage continues a few miles to the south of Asheville, in the town of Flat Rock. The famous poet Carl Sandburg lived for years in Flat Rock, and today his house and farm are a national historic site.

South Carolina comes next. In 1861 the first shots of the Civil War were fired at Fort Sumter, outside Charleston. You can visit Drayton Hall — one of the finest completely unaltered examples Georgian architecture left in the United States — and you can see the more modern USS Yorktown aircraft carrier as well.

The aroma of the past flavors the entire state of South Carolina. The capitol building in the capital city of Columbus bears bronze stars indicating direct hits by canon fire during the Civil War. Woodrow Wilson's boyhood home is a national monument. At the same time, South Carolina sits proudly in the present and gazes optimistically at the future. It is a state with pride, a people filled with spunk, and a legacy overflowing with honor.

In Georgia you will find not only the traces of the great Cherokee and Creek Indian nations — but also the contemporary and cosmopolitan capitol of Atlanta. Antebellum gentility, good old boys, and up-to-the-minute yuppies all exist in Georgia.

Atlanta, one of the most important cities in the United States, sits in the north center part of the state like the brooch on an elegant woman's breast. Originally a Creek Indian settlement called "Standing Peachtree," today greater Atlanta consists of some 83 separate municipalities and is home to nearly two million Americans. The city proper boasts half a million residents.

Atlanta contains 29 colleges and universities, among them Georgia State, Emory, and the world famous Georgia Tech. Coca-Cola — the soft drink which conquered the world, was first served in a small drugstore in Atlanta. Martin Luther King, Jr., was born here, and a two block area of the city is a National Historic District in his memory and honor. There are over 1,700 manufacturing companies, and over 130 banking and financial firms, with offices and factories in greater Atlanta. The airport, Hartsfield Atlanta International Airport, has the largest complex of passenger terminals in the world.

Tourism is Georgia's second largest industry and the famous tourist attraction, Stone Mountain, rises dramatically from the plains 16 miles east of Atlanta. Stone Mountain, the world's largest granite exposure is 825 feet high, and has been carved as a tribute to the Confederacy with the figures of General Robert E. Lee, Andrew "Stonewall" Jackson, and Jefferson Davis riding impressive horses and holding their hats over their hearts as if listening to the anthem of the Confederacy.

Peaches may be Georgia's most famous produce, but Georgia marble is also valued and appreciated around the world. The cotton gin was invented here by Eli Whitney. The state is famous for peanuts and pecans — as well as peaches — and for Plains, the small hometown of America's 39th President, Jimmy Carter.

Savannah — filled with tree-shaded squares and atmospheric historic homes — sits at the top edge of Georgia's coastline, and just below the South Carolina border. Founded in 1733 by General James E. Oglethorpe, Savannah was one of America's major ports for shipping cotton and tobacco to Europe in the years before the Civil War. The antebellum years. Today the city is a major, and very modern, port.

Savannah has the largest historic landmark district of any city in the United States, and over 1,000 historic and architecturally interesting houses and buildings have been lovingly restored to their former grandeur. One of the highlights is the Owens-Thomas House, arguably one of the finest Regency structures in North America. Today you can experience, and almost taste, the flavor of the days before that classic conflict of Blue and Grey by taking a horse-drawn tour past the many historic houses of the old city of Savannah.

About 100 miles south of Savannah, and just below the city of Brunswick sits Jekyll Island, once the location of the unique Jekyll Island Club. The Jekyll Island Club was formed in 1886 by a group of some 60 millionaires who wintered here. The Rockefellers, Goulds, J.P. Morgan, the Vanderbilts, and other very wealthy families and people built fabulous "cottages", some containing scores of rooms. The Jekyll Island Club died when the island was evacuated under direct order by the President (Franklin Delano Roosevelt) during World War II. In 1947 the entire island was sold to the state of Georgia, and today it is a public park. One can still visit a number of the "cottages" and, though the lavish parties are gone, the aroma of the era of the "Robber Barons" still lingers.

At the bottom of Georgia, extending into northern Florida is the ancient and mysterious Okefenokee Swamp, famous for its dark brown water, moss covered cypress trees, and mystical, otherworldly, feeling. The name, Okefenokee, means "land of trembling earth" in the Creek Indian language.

Tennessee is the land of Davy Crockett, Chattanooga (the birthplace of miniature golf), and legendary Nashville. The state bird is the mockingbird.

Nashville, the capital of country music, is also the capital of Tennessee. A thriving and important city it boasts not only hundreds of high quality recording studios — and the icon of the Grand Ole Opry — but also some 707 churches and numerous colleges and universities. Sometimes referred to as the "Athens of the South," Nashville has a full scale reproduction of the Parthenon to reinforce its nickname.

The Grand Ole Opry — the world's largest recording studio with over 4,400 seats — has been broadcasting live country music shows to the world for over sixty years. Since 1925, the Opry has never missed a weekend broadcast, much less a beat.

Tennessee is a long and skinny state, stretching over 500 miles from the banks of the Mississippi River to the western edges of North Carolina. It borders seven states — Virginia, Kentucky, Missouri, Arkansas, Mississippi, Alabama, and Georgia.

Memphis sits at the very southwestern corner of Tennessee, on the banks of the Mississippi River. A major inland port, the city is also the hub of seven separate railroads stretching into the South and the Midwest. Memphis — the name comes from the ancient Egyptian city, and may have been inspired by the similarity of the Mississippi to the Nile — is famous as the home of the "king of rock and roll." Elvis (the Pelvis) Presley began his career in Memphis, and died here. His fantastic and opulent home, Graceland, attracts hundreds of thousands of tourists, visitors, and fans every year. Every August, the city holds a huge celebration in Elvis's honor. Every day, fans weep over Elvis's grave in the Meditation Gardens of Graceland.

The monumental Tennessee Valley Authority dams sit like mammoth mountains over many of the State's rivers. The relatively cheap power they produce may be one of the reasons Tennessee makes more income from manufacturing than from agriculture — one of the few states in the South to do so. The city of Kingsport is a veritable industrial metropolis, with eleven gigantic factories dominating the city's economy. Kingsport Press, a printing firm, may be one of the world's largest printing and book producing facilities.

Kentucky, the "bluegrass state". (The famous bluegrass is only blue for less than two weeks in the Spring, and only looks really blue under the early light of a crisp morning.)

Kentucky's the land of Abraham Lincoln, Daniel Boone, and Henry Clay. Historical home of rugged mountain men and eagle-eyed sharpshooters. A state famous for bourbon, for once wishing to be known as Transylvania — and famous for highbred racing horses.

Lexington, located in the heart of Kentucky's central bluegrass area, is also the epicenter of the elegant horse farms. Over 400 farms raise fillies and train racers in the fields surrounding Lexington. It is the land of gentlemen farmers, multimillion dollar sires, and endless manicured wooden fences.

Louisville (about 70 miles west of Lexington) is Derby town. The first Kentucky Derby was run on May 17, 1875 — and every year since then millions of horse lovers, gamblers, and general bon vivants have, once a year religiously focused their attention and affection on Churchill Downs, the

Victorian track on which the race for the roses is run. The date to remember is the first Saturday in May.

Kentucky is not all horses and bourbon whisky (probably named "bourbon" because the first batch of whisky was distilled out of Kentucky corn by the ruling family in France at the time.) The eastern part of the state is very mountainous, containing the famous Cumberland Gap through which early American adventurers first moved west out of Virginia. On the west there is the "Land Between The Lakes", an inland peninsula 40 miles long.

Kentucky also contains Mammoth Cave National Park — a public park with some 300 miles of interconnected caves buried below the surface. And, here is the military base whose name has entered our popular lexicon to become synonymous with wealth — Fort Knox.

"My Old Kentucky Home", composed by Stephen Foster, is appropriately the official State song. It is a tune we all know, a song which captures not only the sentiments of residents of Kentucky, but also somehow crystallizes every man's nostalgic memories — no matter where you were born or brought up. Some 3.6 million people call Kentucky home today.

The magnolia is the state flower of Mississippi. Soybeans are the principal crop. The river whose name the state bears runs not through the center, but in a wild twisting pattern along its western edge, and the borders of Arkansas and Louisiana.

Cotton was the crop which formed the cornerstone of early commerce and development. William Faulkner — Nobel prize winner, and one of America's most important writers — framed much of the world's impressions of Mississippi. Faulkner, who espoused writing about the eternal truths of "love and honor and pity and pride and compassion and sacrifice" wrote about a mythical country Yoknapatawpha, but he wrote with such obvious insight and from such obviously personal experiences that the world knew Yoknapatawpha must be Mississippi. He penned such magnificent prose, created so many memorable images, and concoted such gut-wrenching plots, that the power of Faulkner's words has flavored impressions of Mississippi ever since.

Jackson, a city of some 200,000 people situated in the center of the State is Mississippi's capital. Named after General Andrew Jackson, the city was designed following a plan penned by Thomas Jefferson, and was the sight of Confederacy President Jefferson Davis's last·public appearance in 1884. Davis's last home was in Biloxi, Mississippi, a port on the north shore of the Gulf of Mexico.

The Casey Jones Railroad museum is in Yazoo City, site of the famous 1900 train wreck. Natchez, an atmospheric city on the banks of the wide Mississippi in the southwestern part of the state, may have more preserved and restored antebellum (before the war, specifically the Civil War) mansions than any city in the South.

Louisiana comes up against the western shore of the Mississippi River, and then cuts a sharp geometric corner out of southwestern Mississippi to control the Gulf Coast, and the land above New Orleans.

New Orleans — famous for wild brass band jazz, the frantic hedonistic fantastic fourteen-day-long festival of Mardi Gras, the ornate ironwork of its architecture, the lazy slightly decadent feeling of the tropics, and much more — sits upon a mass of mud deposited over centuries by the broad Mississippi River.

Approached from the mainland across ribbon-like causeways composed of glimmering bridges, New Orleans looks not so much like the major modern American city it is — but appears a gleaming fictional fantasy island created out of the mind of Walt Disney, or concocted by the fertile imagination of a science fiction writer.

The spires of New Orleans rise from a swamp — the city is banked by levees and bound by the Mississippi River and shallow Lake Pontchtrain. Indeed the soil is so waterlogged that the dead must be buried in crypts above ground. New Orleans is also the city of flowers — bougainvillea, magnolias, gardenias, poinsettias, butterfly lilies, camellias. A city of fantastic flora — live oaks hung with beards of Spanish moss, camphor trees, even Cry Baby trees.

Founded by the French in 1718, New Orleans is a city steeped in history — a community where history, and the passage of time comes up with every step. From the space-age Superdome sports stadium to the ancient buildings of the French Quarter (Vieux Carre), New Orleans makes you realize both the inevitability of decay — and the amazing promise of the future.

The city of "The House of the Rising Sun," the home port of Mississippi River boats and of riverboat gamblers. The famous nightclubs and bars of Bourbon Street. Preservation Hall, the showplace of Dixieland jazz. The land of Creole cooking — Paul Prudhomme, crawfish, spicy gumbo, and catfish soup. Surrounded by the swampy Bayou, with all it's occult mysticism and bad moons rising, New Orleans is funky. It is both very real, and almost imaginary, at the same instant.

New Orleans is the largest city, but Baton Rouge is the capital of Louisiana — a State with a population over four million and covering a land area of approximately 44,000 square miles.

Alabama comes up from the Gulf coast between Mississippi and Florida in a strip about 50 miles across. Above this strip the State widens to a width of some 200 miles.

The thriving port city of Mobile sits at the top of the major bay in bottom of the State. Mobile, founded in 1711 by Jean Baptist LaMoyne, Sieur de Bienville, is one of America's oldest cities. One with a long and varied history. Traces of Mobile's mixed — Spanish, French, and British — heritage still abound in the city.

Just outside Mobile, during battle of Mobile Bay in the Civil War, Admiral Farragut made his famous statement "damn the torpedoes, full speed ahead," as his Union fleet struggled to blockade the port while under fire from forts on both sides of the harbor entrance. Mobile is famous for its azaleas — introduced by a nephew of the founder in the early 18th century — and every year in late February and early April there is the annual Azalea Trail Festival. Thousands of visitors and plant fans come to follow the 35 mile long trail of flowering bushes, and attend the many interrelated celebrations and events.

Montgomery — the first capital city of the Confederacy, and today capital of the State of Alabama — is about 150 miles northeast of Mobile. A bronze star marks the spot on the porch of the Capitol building where Jefferson Davis was sworn in as President of the Confederate States of America on February 18th, 1861. A larger memorial in Oakwood Annex Cemetery marks the grave of country music great Hank Williams.

About 100 miles north of Montgomery is the industrial city of Birmingham, the "Pittsburgh of the South" and home to over a quarter of a million people.

Red Mountain iron ore — long ignored — created Birmingham's steel industry. A monument to this iron and this industry — the famous Vulcan statue showing the Roman god of fire and forge — crowns the top of Red Mountain. This dramatic statue, designed by Giuseppe Moretti for the Louisiana Purchase exposition at St. Louis, was made out of Birmingham iron and cast here. It is the biggest cast iron figure ever created, some 55 feet tall and weighing 60 tones.

At the top of Alabama, nearby to legendary Muscle Shoals, is the town of Tuscumbia, birthplace of Hellen Keller and site of the annual "Coon Dog Toast" on Labor day — a festival featuring Bluegrass music, speech making, buck dancing, and a liars' contest.

The 460-mile-long state of Florida juts out from the southern borders of Alabama and Georgia, separating the Atlantic Ocean from the Gulf of Mexico like a gigantic appendage. The nation's seventh largest state in terms of population, it is home to nearly ten million residents, and the most populated state in the South.

The "sunshine state," Florida leads the world in citrus production, has huge cattle and dairy farms, and a fishing industry which pulls more than 195 million pounds of seafood out of the surrounding oceans every year.

But, Florida's largest industry (as almost everyone knows) is tourism. Nearly 40 million sun and fun seekers from around America and the world pump some three billion dollars into the State's economy every year. The Kennedy Space Center — Florida's fourth largest attraction — receives some two million visitors a year.

Florida is also one of America's oldest discovered areas. St. Augustine, on Florida's northeast coast, is the oldest permanent settlement in the United States, established in 1565 by Pedro Mendez. But, the State's history may go back even before that. It is suspected that Ponce de Leon landed near St. Augustine in 1513 looking for his "fountain of youth." People have been searching for the secret of youth in Florida ever since.

Ownership of the area went back and forth between the Spanish and the English for years. In 1812 a group of Americans took over and declared Florida a separate country. In 1819 Florida joined the Union through a treaty of purchase.

For years Florida was relatively undeveloped. Then, in the early part of this century Henry Morrison Flagler pushed his railroad down the east coast, opening it up to tourists and investors from the North. The result was a real estate boom unmatched in American history.

Golden beaches and tropical palm trees. Alligator alley and the massive marsh of the Everglades with its unique flora and fauna. The Daytona 500 auto race. Jai alai. Polo in Boca Raton. Spring break in Ft. Lauderdale. Hundreds of thousands of boats on the Intracoastal Waterway. Lake Okeechobee, still larger than the State of Delaware though drained to one-third its original size. The shells, star fish, and sea horses of Sanibel and Captiva islands on the west coast. The Thomas Edison winter home and botanical gardens. Walt Disney World. The fabulous mansions of Palm Beach, and the wonderful shopping of Worth Avenue. Over 125 state parks, special feature sights, gardens, preserves, recreation areas, and museums. Florida has something for everyone, an attraction for every taste.

Tallahassee, in the northwestern jog of Florida, is the capital. But, the largest and most famous city — Miami — nestles against the Atlantic Ocean near the very southern tip of the state. Miami, gateway to the Caribbean and South America, is a cultural crucible — a contemporary, cosmopolitan community containing an incredible cross current of influences and interests. From the elegant art deco hotels of Miami beach to the attitudinal postmodern buildings the Arquitectonica design firm, from the retirees playing bridge in the sunshine to the energetic highschool students riding jet-skis across the harbor, it is a city of contrasts and a community of coherence at the same time. Miami, and surrounding Dade county, is both a corner of America — and in many ways its own country.

The phenomenon of the Florida Keys sweeps in an arc from the mainland and Miami 100 miles south into the Gulf of Mexico. An archipelago of 52 islands, the Keys are connected by a single road of 42 bridges — one of the most spectacular over-water drives in the world. In the rich waters surrounding the pearls of the islands are over 600 varieties of fish. One wag has defined the Keys as "bodies of land completely surrounded by fishermen."

This string of islands has always attracted fishermen — along with boisterous buccaneers, artistic eccentrics, lovers of seclusion and of the sea. Ernest Hemingway and John James Audubon, the naturalist and artist, both chose Key West — the southernmost point in the United States — for their homes.

From the fishing fleets of Key West to the rows of white gravestones at Arlington National Cemetery in Virginia, the South is a universe of images, a sea of sensations, and a cosmos of contrasts. The long and languid Mississippi River. The bustle of Birmingham, and the slow pace of afternoons on the front porch. The broad beaches of Florida's Gold Coast. The wet wonder of the Everglades, and the cruel country of the Appalachians. The contemporary crunch of Atlanta, and the antebellum atmosphere of Charleston and Savannah. The dry peanut fields of Georgia, and the water world of the Bayou. The gentility of the plantation owner, and the warm hospitality of the sharecropper. Bourbon, mint juleps, and Sunday morning services. The fantasies of Flagler. The romance of Rhett Butler and Scarlett O'Hara.

"The South is not quite a nation within a nation," says the historian Wilbur Cash, "but it is the next thing to it."

— Michael O'Connor

Old Natchez Trace, near Mount Locust, Mississippi.

Thomas Jefferson's architecture at the University of Virginia.

27

Williamsburg, Virginia — an extensive recreation of a colonial American town filled with meticulously restored buildings, craftspeople working with old techniques, and authentic American flavor.

A colonial kitchen — recreated in all its authentic simplicity — at Stratford Hall Plantation, Stratford, Virginia. The interior of the house of Burgesses at Williamsburg shows the spare but aesthetic style of early American public architecture. An artisan practices the craft of blacksmithing in the authentic fashion at an anvil in colonial Williamsburg.

Monticello, home of one of the most famous
sons of Virginia — Thomas Jefferson — looms in
the mist.

The British redcoats muster in a reenaction of
the Revolutionary war at Colonial Williamsburg.

Crisp rows of clean white tombstones at Arlington Cemetery, Virginia, honor many of the brave soldiers and sons who died in service of the United States. The famous statue of Iwo Jima commemorates the raising of the American flag on that island during World War II.

Tobacco — native to American soil — grows rich and green in many parts of the South. The name (``tobacco'') was originally the Indian word for the pipe used to smoke the dried leaves. It was transferred to the plant itself by early Spanish explorers. Today, tobacco products are a multimillion dollar business.

Rustic Mabry Mill blends beautifully with the riot of autumn leaves on the Blue Ridge Parkway in Virginia.

Colts and adult horses cavort on the bright grass of Spendthrift Farm in central Kentucky.

The white fences of Calumet Farm, Lexington, Kentucky, bask in the glow of the setting sun.

A high-priced, high-performance, thoroughbred horse plunges for the finish line at Churchill Downs, home of the Kentucky Derby.

A trainer puts a thoroughbred through his paces at Keeneland Race Track in Lexington, Kentucky.

A stallion stands proudly in the early morning mist of a horse farm near Paris, Kentucky.

Multi-million dollar stud Seattle Slew rates his own paddock at Spendthrift Farm in Kentucky.

The stately white columns of antebellum plantation houses stare proudly out of their luxuriant surrounding foliage.

Straight trees line the approach to Boone Hall, near Charleston, South Carolina.

From the stately parlor of Shirley Plantation in Virginia to the dining table set for twelve at Linden Plantation, near Natchez Mississippi — the restored rooms of antebellum great houses exude an atmosphere of hospitality, and show a concern for formal Society.

The imposing entrance of Rosalie Plantation, Natchez, Mississippi.

Cotton, the backbone of the Old South.

The broad farmland of Mississippi, as seen from the air.

From a chapel in Oak Ridge to a performer on stage at Opryland in Nashville, Tennessee is study in contrasts.

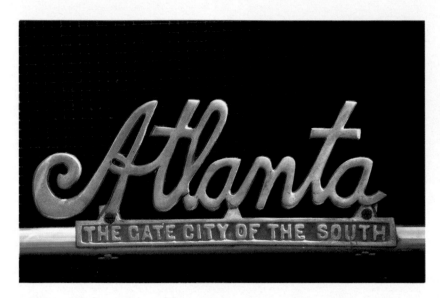

Atlanta — the booming capital of the "sun belt," a bustling modern metropolis filled with commerce and industry. Atlanta is a city where the serious work late — as lighted windows in the Summit Building, and Coca-Cola's international headquarters demonstrate.

From the dramatic multi-story atrium of the Hyatt Regency Hotel, to the bright-white purity of the High Museum of Art — Atlanta is soaring proudly into the future.

A major banking and financial center, Atlanta boasts both the dramatic phoenix of the Federal Reserve Bank and the eclectic juxtaposition of old columns with a modern skyscraper at the Trust Company building.

Swan House, home of the Atlanta Historical Society, brings the past to life through exhibits of maps, memorabilia, and cycloramas depicting Civil War scenes and the city's long history.

The city that never stops keeps going 24 hours a
day at Plaza drugs — even if the immaculate
MARTA public transportation system
occasionally closes.

The dramatic legacy of the Confederacy is honored in all its glory
at Stone Mountain, where the likenesses of Andrew Jackson, Robert E.
Lee, and Jefferson Davis were carved out of the solid granite
hillside with pneumatic power chisels and flame throwers. A nearby
museum shows how it was done, and chronicles the long and convoluted
birth of this amazing monument. Facing page. Cadets on parade at the Citadel.

66

Happy holiday-goers splash through the water at
Six Flags Amusement park in Georgia.

The dark trunks of straight trees in Atlanta's
Tuxedo Park contrast perfectly with a glorious
rainbow of blooming flowers and lush foliage.

Spring flowers cover a hillside in Georgia.

WALTER McELREATH MEMORIAL

THE ATLANTA
HISTORICAL SOCIETY

Swan House, built in 1928 and home of the Atlanta Historical Society.

The Martin Luther King Memorial in Atlanta.

The Cathedral of St. John the Baptist, Savannah.

Savannah, Georgia — famous for its lovingly restored old houses and numerous lush parks and squares.

The lush foliage of Victoria Drive and the 1828 main house of Wormsloe, Savannah.

A group of bright-eyed girls peer down from the porch of Ashley Hall.

A colorful paddlewheeler steams up the Mississippi near New Orleans.

The powerful paddlewheel of the "Mississippi Queen."

A riverboat churns the water as it chugs forward on the Mississippi.

The famous "Delta Queen" — and its magnificently opulent grand staircase.

An ornate cast-iron balcony in the French Quarter of New Orleans.

Jackson Brewery, New Orleans.

A jazz funeral in New Orleans, where the band plays on in memory of the departed.

Throngs of revelers crowd Bourbon Street during Mardi Gras in New Orleans.

93

One costumed reveler casts baleful eyes through a veil of bright ribbons during the Mardi Gras festival.

Two masked clowns strike a pose for the photographer on Bourbon Street during Fat Tuesday, the mad culmination of the two-week-long Mardi Gras festival.

95

Bourbon Street — home of brass band jazz — where the horns wail and musicians improvise in smokey back rooms.

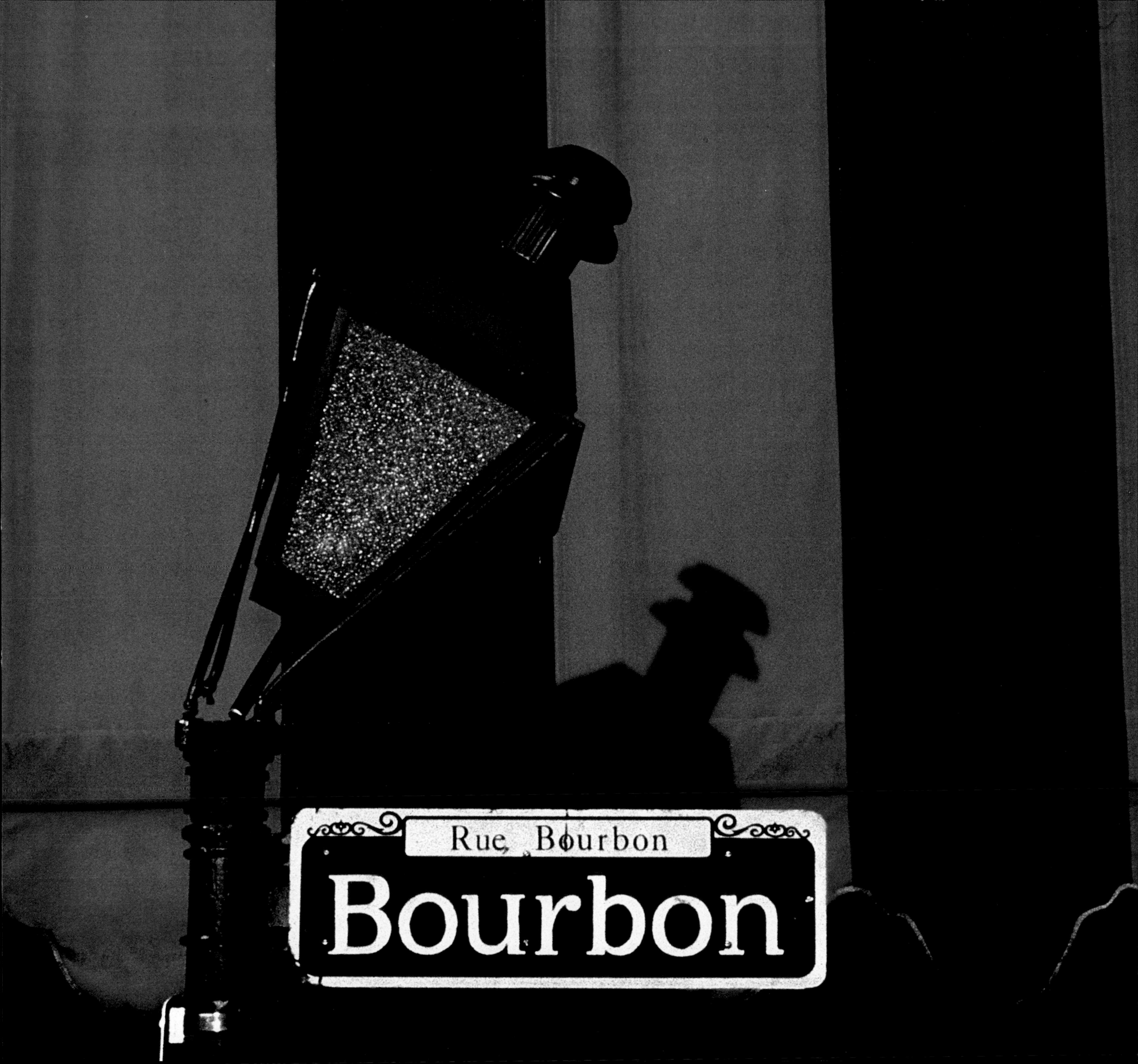
Rue Bourbon
Bourbon

A young member of a New Orleans marching band follows in the soulful footsteps of earlier jazz musicians.

Dramatic fireworks burst in the night sky over the bright lights of the 1984 New Orleans World's Fair.

Architect Charles Moore created
this fantastic postmodern
"Piazza d'Italia" for the 1984
World's Fair in New Orleans.
It still stands.

Ida Kohlmeyer created this equally fantastical "Krew of Polydras"

105

The annual Mardi Gras festival — leading up to Ash Wednesday and the beginning of Lent — brings out incredible costumes and amazing floats for the parades. The Jazz Heritage Festival brings out the best of the marching jazz bands, often attired in equally dazzling outfits.

Inside, the Superdome sports and entertainment stadium covers acres of ground — enough for an entire football field. From the outside, it appears a gigantic mystical monument basking in the golden glow of sunset.

Bourbon Street, New Orleans.

Armstrong amusement park.

Ripe oranges hang heavy on the
trees of a Florida citrus grove.

A South Carolina dogwood tree
— glorious in full flower during the Spring.

A country road twists through the
rich farmland near Tahula, Mississippi.

A lily pond near Panama City, Florida, reflects the beautiful colors of sunset.

Working boats sit docked on a back stream in the wet world of the Bayou.

A lone house stands out against the vast marsh and many streams of southern Louisiana.

Real flamingos — not the cast concrete kind — in captivity at Busch Gardens near Tampa, Florida, and wild in the Florida keys.

Walt Disney World, Florida.

Fantasyland, Walt Disney World, Florida — land of dreams, stories, and cartoon characters, is dominated by the 18-story Cinderella Castle.

The gigantic geodesic dome — symbol of Epcot Center, one part of Walt Disney World, the most popular tourist attraction in the world.

127

An old steam-powered train — gas lamp and all — at Walt Disney World.

The neon lights of the Kodak Pavilion, Epcot Center.

The supermodern monorail runs visitors around Walt Disney World.

The World Showcase at Walt Disney World — where you can go from Japan to Venice to China with ease and within a few minutes.

Florida's famous beaches — warm waves breaking on miles of white sand — attract millions of sun worshipers every year.

Alvarez House in St. Augustine, Florida — a national historic landmark which may the oldest house still standing in the United States.

The laboratory at Thomas Edison's winter home near Ft. Meyers, Florida — preserved just the way it was when he worked there.

A pair of palm trees stand proudly against a bright blue sky on the white sand of a Florida beach.

Expensive power boats — some 60,000 of them — cruise and dock on the Intercoastal waterway and adjoining canals in greater Fort Lauderdale, Florida.

Earlier rockets and the space shuttle "Discovery" at the
Kennedy Space Center, Florida.

144

The eccentric and interesting Art Deco buildings of Miami Beach — a national historic district, and a riot of pastel colors and whimsical, stylish fantasy.

A newer condominium on Miami Beach picks up the colors and the ideas of the older Deco buildings.

"Streamlined Moderne," curved corners, soaring fluted columns — all painted in bright pastel colors and under a pure blue sky — these are some of the signatures of Miami Beach's valuable Art Deco buildings.

154

The glorious, stylish, fun, pastel facades of two Art Deco hotels in Miami Beach.

155

A windsurfer strains to hold his sail against the wind on the water off one of Florida's magnificent beaches.

An Art Deco style hotel in Fort Lauderdale.

The "Greystone Hotel" in Miami Beach.

Villa Vizcaya — an ornate Italian Renaissance-style mansion built by industrial tycoon James Deering — contains 72 opulent rooms filled with rare European and Oriental furniture and accessories. Now a museum, Vizcaya's gardens and main house are open to the public.

The formal gardens, and Venice-like docks, of Villa Vizcaya.

Villa Vizcaya.

Elevated causeways and bridges connect the islands of the Florida Keys like silken treads tying together a string of precious pearls.

Hemingway House, Key West, Florida.

The porch and fountain at Hemingway House, Key West.

The casual lifestyle of Key West.

Southern Florida flora.

Index of Photographers

The southernmost house in the United States, Key West, Florida.